Truth with a Mission

Mission

Reading Scripture Missiologically

Christopher J H Wright

International Ministries Director,
Langham Partnership International

GROVE BOOKS LIMITED
RIDLEY HALL RD CAMBRIDGE CB3 9HU

Contents

The Cover Illustration is by Peter Ashton

The material here (in various modifications) was first an occasional paper of All Nations Christian College, then published for the Fourth National Evangelical Anglican Congress in Paul Gardner, Chris Wright and Chris Green (ed), *Fanning the Flame: Bible, Cross and Mission* (Grand Rapids: Zondervan, 2003), then expanded in Craig Bartholomew (et al, ed), *Out of Egypt: Biblical Theology and Biblical Interpretation*, (Grand Rapids: Zondervan, and Carlisle: Paternoster, 2004), and forms the core argument for a greatly expanded book on missional hermeneutics of Scripture, *God's Mission, God's World and God's People* (Downers Grove: InterVarsity Press, forthcoming).

The word 'hermeneutic' comes from the Greek word meaning 'to translate' (for instance, in John 1.41) or 'to interpret' (Luke 24.27), and is used to refer to the process of interpreting or reading texts, primarily in relation to how we make sense of them in our own context. In this study, Israel's God is referred to as Yahweh, the traditional translation of the four-letter name YHWH (sometimes known as the 'tetragrammaton').

All the royalties from this book have been assigned to Langham Literature, a programme of the Langham Partnership International, founded by John Stott. Chris Wright is the International Ministries Director. For further information visit the website at www.langhampartnership.org

First Impression December 2005
ISSN 1365-490X
ISBN 1 85174 608 0

Introduction

'Go ye into all the world and preach the gospel to every creature,' they urged me, along with other similar imperatives in glowing gothic calligraphy.

I remember them so vividly from my childhood—the great banner texts around the walls of the missionary conventions in Northern Ireland where I would help my father at the stall of the Unevangelized Fields Mission, of which he was Irish Secretary after twenty years in Brazil. By the age of twelve I could have quoted you all the key texts—'Go ye therefore and make disciples,' 'How shall they hear?,' 'You shall be my witnesses…to the ends of the earth,' 'Whom shall we send?…Here am I, send me.' I knew my missionary Bible verses. I had responded to many a rousing sermon on most of them.

By the age of twenty-one I had a degree in theology from Cambridge in which the same texts had been curiously lacking. At least, it is curious to me now. At the time there seemed to be little connection at all between theology and mission in the mind of the lecturers, or of myself, or, for all I knew, in the mind of God either. 'Theology' was all about God—what God was like, what God had said and done, and what mostly dead people had speculated on such questions. 'Mission' was about us, the living, and what we have been doing since Carey (who, of course, was the first missionary, we so erroneously thought). Or more precisely, mission is what we evangelicals do since we are the ones who know that the Bible has told us (or some of us, at least) to go and be missionaries.

'Mission is what we do.' That was the assumption, supported of course by clear biblical commands. 'Jesus sends me, this I know, for the Bible tells me so.' Many years later, including years when I was teaching theology myself as a missionary in India, I found myself teaching a module called *The Biblical Basis of Mission* at All Nations Christian College—an international mission training institution.[1] The module title itself embodies the same assumption. Mission is the noun, the given reality. It is

'Mission is what we do' —that was the assumption, supported of course by clear biblical commands

something we do and we basically know what it is. And the reason why we know we should be doing it, the basis, foundation or grounds on which we justify it, must be found in the Bible. As good evangelicals we need a biblical basis for everything we do. What, then, is the biblical basis for mission? Roll out the texts. Add some that nobody else has thought of. Do some joined up theology. Add some motivational fervour. And the class is heart-warmingly appreciative. Now they have even more biblical support for what they already believed anyway, for these are All Nations students, after all. They only came because they are committed to doing mission.

I wanted them to see that the whole Bible is itself a 'missional' phenomenon

This mild caricature is not in the least derogatory in intent. I believe passionately that mission is what we should be doing, and I believe the Bible endorses and mandates it. However, the more I taught that course, the more I used to introduce it by telling the students that I would like to rename it—from *The Biblical Basis of Mission,* to *The Missional Basis of the Bible.'* I wanted them to see not just that the Bible contains a number of texts which happen to provide a rationale for missionary endeavour but that *the whole Bible is itself a 'missional' phenomenon.*

Questions for Reflection

What in the Bible has encouraged you to take mission seriously—particular passages, or themes, or aspects of the character of God—or what?

How has your understanding of the nature and importance of mission changed? What has brought about this change—experience, the reflection of others, or your reading of Scripture?

How have changes in your understanding of mission changed the way you read the Bible?

The Bible as the Product of God's Mission

2

A missional hermeneutic of the Bible begins with the Bible's very existence.

For those who affirm some relationship (however articulated) between these texts and the self-revelation of our creator God, the whole canon of Scripture is a missional phenomenon in the sense that it witnesses to the self-giving movement of this God towards his creation and towards us, human beings in God's own image, but wayward and wanton. The writings which now comprise our Bible are themselves the product of, and witness to, the ultimate mission of God.

> The very existence of the Bible is incontrovertible evidence of the God who refused to forsake his rebellious creation, who refused to give up, who was and is determined to redeem and restore fallen creation to his original design for it...The very existence of such a collection of writings testifies to a God who breaks through to human beings, who disclosed himself to them, who will not leave them unilluminated in their darkness...who takes the initiative in re-establishing broken relationships with us.[2]

Furthermore, the processes by which these texts came to be written were often profoundly missional in nature. Many of them emerged out of events, or struggles, or crises, or conflicts, in which the people of God engaged with the constantly changing and challenging task of articulating and living out their understanding of God's revelation and redemptive action in the world. Sometimes these were struggles internal to the people of God themselves; sometimes they were highly polemical struggles with competing religious claims and worldviews that surrounded them.

So a missional reading of such texts is very definitely not a matter of, *first*, finding the 'real' meaning by objective exegesis, and only then, *secondly*, cranking up some 'missiological implications' as a homiletic supplement to the 'text itself.' Rather, it is to see how a text often has its origin in some issue, need, controversy or threat, which the people of God needed to address in the context of their mission. The text in itself is a product of mission in action.

This is easily demonstrated in the case of the New Testament.[3] Most of Paul's letters were written in the heat of his missionary efforts: wrestling with the theological basis of the inclusion of the gentiles; affirming the need for Jew and gentile to accept one another in Christ and in the church; tackling the baffling range of new problems that assailed young churches as the gospel took root in the world of Greek polytheism; confronting incipient heresies with clear affirmations of the supremacy and sufficiency of Jesus Christ, and so on.

And why were the gospels so-called? Because they were written to explain the significance of the *evangel*—the good news about Jesus of Nazareth, especially his death and resurrection. Confidence in these things was essential to the missionary task of the expanding church. And the person to whom we owe the largest quantity of the New Testament, Luke, shapes his two volume work in such a way that the missionary mandate to the disciples to be Christ's witnesses to the nations comes as the climax to volume one and the introduction to volume two.

Texts of Engagement

But also in the case of the Old Testament we can see that many of these texts emerged out of the engagement of Israel with the surrounding world in the light of the God they knew in their history and in covenantal relationship. People produced texts in relation to what they believed God had done, was doing, or would do, in their world.

- The **Torah** records the exodus as an act of Yahweh that comprehensively confronted and defeated the power of Pharaoh and all his rival claims to deity and allegiance. It presents a theology of creation that stands in sharp contrast to the polytheistic creation myths of Mesopotamia.

- The **historical narratives** portray the long and sorry story of Israel's struggle with the culture and religion of Canaan, a struggle reflected also in the pre-exilic prophets.

- **Exilic and post-exilic** texts emerge out of the task that the small remnant community of Israel faced to define their continuing identity as a community of faith in successive empires of varying hostility or tolerance.

- **Wisdom** texts interact with international wisdom traditions in the surrounding cultures, but do so with staunch monotheistic disinfectant.

- And in **worship and prophecy**, Israelites reflect on the relationship between their God, Yahweh, and the rest of the nations—sometimes negatively, sometimes positively—and on the nature of their own role as Yahweh's elect priesthood in their midst.

The Bible, then, is a missional phenomenon in itself. The writings which now comprise our Bible are themselves the product of, and witness to, the ultimate mission of God. The individual texts within it often reflect the struggles of being a people with a mission in a world of competing cultural and religious claims. And the canon eventually consolidates the recognition that it is through these texts that the people whom God has called to be his own (in both Testaments), has been shaped as a community of memory and hope, a community of mission, failure and striving.

In short, a missional hermeneutic proceeds from the assumption that the whole Bible renders to us the story of God's mission through God's people in their engagement with God's world for the sake of God's purpose for the whole of God's creation. Mission is not just one of a list of things that the Bible happens to talk about, only a bit more urgently than some. Mission is, in that much-abused phrase, 'what it's all about.'

Questions for Reflection

Reflect on your own story of coming to faith. What elements of that story reflect the missionary outreach of God to you?

In what ways does your story correspond to the missional shape of the scriptural story?

What words of Scripture would you draw on in telling your story? How do the different elements of the scriptural story (creation, law, story, exile, wisdom, worship, prophecy) find their place in your story?

3 Reading the Scriptures with the Risen Christ

Now to say 'mission is what the Bible is all about' is a bold claim. I would not expect to be able to turn any phrase that began 'the biblical basis of...' around the other way.

There is, for example, a biblical basis for marriage, but there is not, I presume, 'a marital basis for the Bible.' There is a biblical basis for work, but work is not 'what the Bible is all about.' However, I take some encouragement for my claim from an impeccable authority. It seems to me that Jesus comes very close to saying, 'This is what the Bible is all about,' when he gave his disciples their final lecture in Old Testament hermeneutics. 'This is what is written,' he said. 'The Christ will suffer and rise from the dead on the third day, and repentance and forgiveness of sins will be preached in his name to all nations, beginning in Jerusalem' (Luke 24.46–47).

It seems to me that Jesus comes very close to saying, 'This is what the Bible is all about'

Now Jesus is not quoting a specific text here, though we would love to have been able to ask which Scriptures he particularly had in mind. (Doubtless, the two from Emmaus could have filled in the gaps). The point is that he includes the whole of this sentence under the heading, 'this is what is written.' He seems to be saying that the whole of the Scripture (which we now know as the Old Testament) finds its focus and fulfilment *both* in the life and death and resurrection of Israel's Messiah *and* in the mission to all nations, which flows out from that event. Luke tells us that with these words Jesus 'opened their minds so they could understand the Scriptures' or, as we might put it, he was setting their hermeneutical orientation and agenda. The proper way for disciples of Jesus of Nazareth (crucified and risen) to read their Scriptures is *messianically* and *missiologically.*

Paul, though he was not present for the Old Testament hermeneutics lecture on the day of resurrection, clearly had his own way of reading his Scriptures radically transformed in exactly the same way with the same double focus. Testifying before Festus he declares, 'I am saying nothing beyond what the prophets and Moses said would happen — that the Messiah would suffer and, as the first to rise from the dead, would proclaim light *to his own people and to the nations'* (Acts 26.22–23). It was this dual understanding of the Scriptures which had then shaped Paul's whole CV as the apostle of the Messiah Jesus to the gentiles.

On the whole, evangelicals have been good at the former (messianic reading of the Old Testament) but inadequate with the latter (missiological reading of it). We read the Old Testament messianically in the light of Jesus, in the sense of finding in it a whole messianic theology and eschatology which we see as fulfilled in Jesus. In doing so we follow his own example, of course, and that of his first followers and the authors of the gospels. But what we have so often failed to do is to go beyond the mere satisfaction of ticking off so-called messianic predictions that have 'been fulfilled.' And we have failed to go further because we have not grasped the missiological significance of the Messiah.

We have failed to go further because we have not grasped the missiological significance of the Messiah

Reading with the Promised One

The Messiah was the promised one who would embody in his own person the identity and mission of Israel, as their representative, king, leader and saviour. Through the Messiah as his anointed agent, Yahweh the God of Israel would bring about all that he intended for Israel. But what was that mission of Israel? Nothing less than to be 'a light to the nations,' the means of bringing the redemptive blessing of God to all the nations of the world, as originally promised in the title deeds of the covenant with Abraham. For the God of Israel is also the creator God of all the world. Through the Messiah, therefore, the God of Israel would also bring about all that he intended for the nations. The eschatological redemption and restoration of Israel would issue in the ingathering of the nations. The full meaning of recognizing Jesus as Messiah, then, lies in recognizing also his role in relation to the mission of Israel for the sake of the nations. Hence, a messianic reading of the Old Testament has to flow on to a missiological reading—which is precisely the connection that Jesus makes in Luke 24.

However, even if we accept that Jesus offers us a messiah-focused and mission-generating hermeneutic of the Scriptures, we may still query the claim that somehow there is a missional hermeneutic of the whole Bible such that 'mission is what it's all about.' This uneasiness stems from the persistent, almost subconscious paradigm that mission is fundamentally 'something we do.' This is especially so if we fall into the evangelical reductionist habit of using the word 'mission' or 'missions' as more or less synonymous with evangelism. Quite clearly the whole Bible is not just 'about evangelism,' even though evangelism is certainly a fundamental part of biblical mission as entrusted to us. Evangelism *is* something we do and it *is* validated by clear biblical imperatives. The appropriateness of speaking of 'a missional basis of the Bible' becomes apparent only when we shift our paradigm of mission from *our* human agency to the ultimate purposes of *God* himself. For clearly the Bible is, in some sense, 'all about God.' What, then, does it mean to talk of the mission of God?

Questions for Reflection

To what extent do you read the Old Testament as 'simply' predicting the coming of Jesus?

Is this adequate in the light of the missional shape of the Bible?

What might it mean to read the Old Testament as a missional document whose missional aim is fulfilled in the person of Jesus?

Whose Mission is it Anyway? 4

God with a Mission

Though the phrase *Missio Dei* has been misused in some theology virtually to exclude evangelism, it does express a major biblical truth. The God revealed in the Scriptures is personal, purposeful and goal orientated. The opening account of creation portrays God working towards a goal, completing it with satisfaction and resting, content with the result. And from the great promise of God to Abraham in Genesis 12.1–3 we know this God to be totally, covenantally, eternally committed to the mission of blessing the nations through the agency of the people of Abraham. From that point on, the mission of God could be summed up in the words of the hymn, 'God is working his purpose out as year succeeds to year,' and as generations come and go.

The Bible presents itself to us fundamentally as a narrative, a historical narrative at one level, but a grand, meta-narrative at another. It begins with a God of purpose in creation; moves on to the conflict and problem generated by human rebellion against that purpose; spends most of its narrative journey in the story of God's redemptive purposes being worked out on the stage of human history; and finishes beyond the horizon of its own history with the eschatological hope of a new creation. This has often been presented as a four-point narrative—creation, fall, redemption and future hope. This whole world-view is predicated on teleological monotheism—that is, there is one God at work in the universe and in human history, and that God has a goal, a purpose, a mission which will ultimately be accomplished by the power of his word and for the glory of his name. This is the mission of the biblical God.

To read the whole Bible in the light of this great over-arching perspective of the mission of God is to read 'with the grain' of this whole collection of Scriptures that constitute our canon. This foundational point is a key assumption of 'a missiological hermeneutic' of the Bible. It is nothing more than to accept that the biblical worldview locates us in the midst of a narrative of the universe behind which stands the mission

The biblical worldview locates us in the midst of a narrative of the universe behind which stands the mission of the living God

of the living God. All creation will render 'glory to the Father and to the Son and to the Holy Spirit, as it was in the beginning, is now, and ever shall be.' That is a missional perspective.

Humanity with a Mission

On the day of their creation, human beings were given their mission on the planet so purposefully prepared for their arrival—the mandate to fill the earth and subdue it and to rule over the rest of creation (Genesis 1.28). This delegated authority within the created order is moderated by the parallel commands in the complementary account, 'to serve and to keep' the garden (Genesis 2.15). The care and keeping of creation is our human mission. We are on the planet with a purpose that flows from the creative purpose of God himself. Out of this understanding of our humanity (which is also teleological, like our doctrine of God) flows our ecological responsibility, our economic activity involving work, productivity, exchange and trade, and the whole cultural mandate.

To be human is to have a purposeful role in God's creation

To be human is to have a purposeful role in God's creation. In relation to that creational mission, Christians need to be reminded that God holds us accountable to himself for our humanity as much as for our Christianity. There is, therefore, a legitimate place for ecological concern and action, for biblical earth-keeping, within our understanding of Christian mission responsibility—on the assumption that Christians too are humans made in the image of God (indeed being restored even more fully to that humanity in Christ), who have not been given some privileged exemption from the mission God entrusted to our whole species. This ecological dimension of our mission flows not only from creation, but also reflects an eschatological perspective. The biblical vision is of a new creation, of which Christ is the heir. Our care for the earth is an expression of our understanding of its future as well as its origin (similarly to our concern for the human person).

Israel with a Mission

Against the background of human sin and rebellion, described in the bleak narratives of Genesis 3–11, running from the disobedience of Adam and Eve to the building of the tower of Babel, God initiates his redemptive mission of blessing the nations of humanity, beginning with the call of Abraham in Genesis 12. This is the essential missional purpose of God's election of Israel. Israel came into existence as a people with a mission entrusted from God for the sake of the rest of the nations. All that Israel was, or was supposed to be

—all that Yahweh their God did in them, for them and through them—was ultimately linked to this wider purpose of God for the nations.

A missiological hermeneutic of the Old Testament, in its redemptive dimension, centres around this point. Israel's election was not a rejection of other nations but was explicitly for the sake of all nations. This universality of God's purpose that embraces the particularity of God's chosen means is a recurrent theme. Though not always explicitly present, it is never far from the surface of the way in which Scripture portrays Israel's intended self-understanding. We shall explore this missiological reading of the Old Testament more fully below.

Jesus with a Mission

Jesus did not just arrive. He had a very clear conviction that he was sent. But even before Jesus was old enough to have clear convictions about anything, his significance was recognized. Just as Luke ends his gospel with the double significance of Jesus for Israel and for the world, so also right at the start he makes the same connection. It is there in the words of recognition spoken by Simeon as he cradled the infant Jesus, words appreciated by generations of Anglicans for their evening beauty in the *Nunc dimittis*, but rarely recognized for the missiological significance of their double messianic claim, 'Lord now let your servant depart in peace, according to your word. For my eyes have seen your salvation, which you have prepared in the sight of *all people*, to be a light for revelation to *the nations* and for glory to your people *Israel*' (Luke 2.29–32).

It was at his baptism that Jesus receives an affirmation of his true identity and mission. The voice of his Father at his baptism combined the identity of the Servant figure in Isaiah (echoing the phraseology of Isaiah 42.1), and that of the Davidic messianic king (echoing the affirmation of Psalm 2.7). Both of these dimensions of his identity and role were energized with a sense of mission. The mission of the Servant was both to restore Israel to Yahweh and also to be the agent of God's salvation reaching to the ends of the earth (Isaiah 49.6). The mission of the Davidic messianic king was both to rule over a redeemed Israel according to the agenda of many prophetic texts, and also to receive the nations and the ends of the earth as his heritage (Psalm 2.8).

Jesus' sense of mission (the aims, motivation and self-understanding behind his recorded words and actions) has been a matter of intense scholarly discussion. What seems very clear is that Jesus built his own agenda on what he perceived to be the agenda of his Father. His will was to do his Father's will. God's mission determined his. In the obedience of Jesus, even to death, the mission of God reached its climax.

The Church with a Mission

As our quotation of Luke 24 above indicated, Jesus entrusted to the church a mission which is directly rooted in his own identity, passion and victory as the crucified and risen Messiah. Jesus immediately followed the text quoted with the words, 'You are witnesses'—a mandate repeated in Acts 1.8, 'You will be my witnesses.' It is almost certain that Luke intends us to hear in this an echo of the same words spoken by Yahweh to Israel in Isaiah 43.10–12.

> You are my witnesses, declares the LORD, and my servant whom I have chosen,
> So that you may know and believe me and understand that I am he.
> Before me no god was formed nor will there be one after me.
> I, even I, am the LORD, and apart from me there is no saviour.
> I have revealed and saved and proclaimed—I, and not some foreign god among you.
> You are my witnesses, declares the LORD, that I am God.

Israel knew the identity of the true and living God; therefore they were entrusted with bearing witness to that in a world of nations and their gods. The disciples know the true identity of the crucified and risen Jesus; therefore they are entrusted with bearing witness to that to the ends of the earth. Mission flows from the identity of God and his Christ.

Paul goes further and identifies the mission of his own small band of church planters with the international mission of the Servant, quoting Isaiah 49.6 in Acts 13.47 and saying quite bluntly, '[T]his is what the Lord has commanded *us*: "I have made you a light for the nations, that you may bring salvation to the ends of the earth."'[4] So again, the mission of the church flows from the mission of God and the fulfilment of his purposes and his word. It is not so much, as someone has said, that God has a mission for his church in the world, as that God has a church for his mission in the world. Mission is not just something we do (though it certainly includes that). Mission, from the point of view of our human endeavour, means the committed participation of God's people in the purposes of God for the redemption of the whole creation. Mission, like salvation, belongs to our God and to the Lamb. We are those who are called to share in its accomplishment.

The mission of the church flows from the mission of God and the fulfilment of his purposes and his word

Putting these perspectives together, then, and summarizing what I have said above, a missiological hermeneutic means that we seek to read any part of the Bible:

- in the light of God's purpose for his whole creation, including the redemption of humanity and the creation of the new heavens and new earth;

- in the light of God's purpose for human life in general on the planet, and of all the Bible teaches about human culture, relationships, ethics and behaviour;

- in the light of God's historical election of Israel, their identity and role in relation to the nations, and the demands he made on their worship, social ethics and total value system;

- in the light of the centrality of Jesus of Nazareth, his messianic identity and mission in relation to Israel and the nations, his cross and resurrection;

- in the light of God's calling of the church, the community of believing Jews and gentiles who constitute the extended people of the Abraham covenant, to be the agent of God's blessing to the nations in the name and for the glory of the Lord Jesus Christ.

Questions for Reflection

'We should not be concerned about [for example] politics or the environment, since the most important thing is to see people come to faith in Jesus, and we should put all our energies into this and not get distracted.' How would you answer this, in the light of what Scripture says about mission?

What were the things that led Israel away from fulfilling its mission under God? In what ways has the Christian church done similar things?

What aspects do you see in Jesus' approach to his mission that might help our own understanding of mission?

How might Paul's missionary strategy give us insights into being effective in our mission?

5

A Missiological Perspective on the Old Testament

Evangelical Christians have traditionally had less of a problem reading the New Testament from a missional angle.

This is hardly surprising given the dominance within the New Testament of the apostle Paul and his missionary travels and writings. So in the rest of this essay I want to focus on how the above proposals can help us to develop a missiological reading of the Old Testament.

Preaching mission from the Old Testament usually rouses people's curiosity, mainly because it is unexpected

Certainly, *preaching* mission from the Old Testament usually rouses people's curiosity, mainly because it is unexpected. Many people, in my frequent experience, are surprised to hear a sermon on mission based on a text from the Old Testament. 'Mission' is widely viewed as a task originating from some words of Jesus on the Mount of Ascension. It seems to involve sending off somewhat peculiar but doubtless very worthy people to far-off parts of the earth to work for God in a bewildering variety of ways, and then to return from time to time to tell us about their adventures and ask for continued support. Since nothing of that sort seems to have happened in the Old Testament (not even Jonah came home on furlough to raise funds for a return trip to Nineveh), mission is deemed 'missing—presumed unborn' in that era.

A more sophisticated form of such a caricature is to be found in the way David Bosch in his magisterial survey, *Transforming Mission*, relegates the Old Testament's contribution on mission to a sub-section of a chapter entitled 'Reflections on the New Testament as a Missionary Document.'[5] The Old Testament certainly provides essential theological preparation for the emerging mission of the New Testament church, but Bosch defines mission in terms of crossing barriers for the sake of the gospel (barriers of geography, culture, language, religion, and so on). Since Israel received no mandate to *go to* the nations in that sense, there is, in Bosch's view, no mission in the Old Testament.

Apart from observing that in fact there are many 'barrier-crossing' episodes in the grand Old Testament story of Israel's journey with Yahweh which are worthy of missiological reflection, I would argue that Bosch has defined mission too narrowly. What follows is a brief survey of some of the key Old Testament themes, which contribute to the broadening of the idea of mission which I have argued for above. This is, to be clear once again, not a search for bits of the Old Testament that might say something relevant to our narrowed concept of sending missionaries, but rather a sketch of some of the great trajectories of Israel's understanding of their God and his mission through them and for the world. We are not concerned about how the Old Testament gives incidental support to what we already do, but with the theology that undergirds the whole worldview that Christian mission assumes.

We are concerned with the theology that undergirds the whole worldview that Christian mission assumes

What we will merely sketch below are the missiological implications of four major pillars of Old Testament faith — monotheism, election, ethics and eschatology. A great deal more could be fruitfully explored in the same way.

The Uniqueness and Universality of Yahweh

According to the Old Testament texts, the faith of Israel made remarkable affirmations about Yahweh, affirmations which had a polemical edge in their own context and still stand as distinctive claims. Among them are the declaration that Yahweh alone is God and there is no other (for example, Deut 4.35, 39). As sole deity, it is Yahweh, therefore, who owns the world and runs the world (Deut 10.14, 27; Psalm 24.1; Jer 27.1–12; 1 Chron 29.11). This ultimately means the radical displacement of all other rival gods and that Yahweh is God over the whole earth and all nations (for example, Psalm 96; Jer 10.1–16; Isaiah 43.9–13; 44.6–20). The impact of these claims is felt in such widely varying contexts as the struggle against idolatry, the language of worship and the response to other nations, both in their own contemporary international history, and in eschatological vision.

There is no doubt that the strength of the Old Testament affirmations about the uniqueness and universality of Yahweh as God underlie, and indeed provide some of the vocabulary for, the New Testament affirmations about the uniqueness and universality of Jesus (see also Phil 2.9–11, based on Isaiah 45.23; and 1 Cor 8.5–6, based on Deut 6.4). It is also noteworthy that these early Christian affirmations were equally polemical in their own historical context as those of ancient Israel and in turn provided the primary rationale and motivation for Christian mission. We are dealing here with the missiological implications of biblical monotheism.

A fully biblical understanding of the universality and uniqueness of Yahweh and of Jesus Christ stands in the frontline of a missiological response to the relativism at the heart of religious pluralism and some forms of postmodern philosophy.

Yahweh's Election of Israel for the Purpose of Blessing the Nations

The Old Testament begins on the stage of universal history. After the accounts of creation we read the story of God's dealings with fallen humanity and the problem and challenge of the world of the nations (Genesis 1–11). After the stories of the Flood and of the Tower of Babel, could there be any future for the nations in relation to God? Or would judgment have to be God's final word?

The creator God has a purpose, a goal, and it is nothing less than blessing the nations of humanity

The story of Abraham, beginning in Genesis 12, gives a clear answer. God's declared commitment is that he intends to bring blessing to the nations, 'all the families of the earth will be blessed through you' (Genesis 12.3). Repeated six times in Genesis alone, this key affirmation is the foundation of biblical mission, inasmuch as it presents the mission of God. The creator God has a purpose, a goal, and it is nothing less than blessing the nations of humanity. So fundamental is this divine agenda that Paul defines the Genesis declaration as 'the gospel in advance' (Gal 3.8). And the concluding vision of the whole Bible signifies the fulfilment of the Abrahamic promise, as people from every nation, tribe, language and people are gathered among the redeemed in the new creation (Rev 7.9). The gospel and mission both begin in Genesis, then, and both are located in the redemptive intention of the Creator to bless the nations. Mission is God's address to the problem of fractured humanity. And God's mission is universal in its ultimate goal and scope.

The same Genesis texts which affirm the universality of God's mission to bless the nations also, and with equal strength, affirm the particularity of God's election of Abraham and his descendants to be the vehicle of that mission. The election of Israel is assuredly one of the most fundamental pillars of the biblical worldview, and of Israel's historical sense of identity.[6] It is vital to insist that although the belief in their election could be (and was) distorted into a narrow doctrine of national superiority, that move was resisted in Israel's own literature (for example, Deut 7.7ff). The affirmation is that Yahweh, the God who had chosen Israel, was also the creator, owner and Lord of the whole world (Deut 10.14f, see also Exodus 19.4–6). That is, he was not just 'their God'—he was God of all (as Paul hammers home in Romans 4). Yahweh had chosen Israel in relation to his purpose for the world, not just for Israel. The election of Israel was not tantamount to a rejection of the nations, but explicitly for their ultimate benefit. If we might paraphrase John, in a way he would probably have accepted, 'God so loved the world that he chose Israel.'

Thus, rather than asking if Israel itself 'had a mission,' in the sense of being 'sent' anywhere (anachronistically injecting our 'sending missionaries' paradigm again), we need to see the missional nature of Israel's existence in relation to the mission of God in the world. Israel's mission was *to be* something, not *to go* somewhere. This perspective is clearly focused in the person of the Servant of Yahweh, who both embodies the election of Israel (identical things are said about Israel and the Servant), and also is charged with the mission (like Israel's) of bringing the blessing of Yahweh's justice, salvation and glory to the ends of the earth.

The Ethical Dimension of Israel's 'Visibility' Among the Nations

Naturally, then, there is an enormous amount of interest in the Old Testament around the way in which Israel related to the nations. It is far from being a simple relationship. On the one hand, there is the ultimate vision of Israel being a blessing to the nations. On the other hand, there is the calling for Israel to be separate from them, to resist their idolatry, to avoid their wickedness, to reject their gods and their ways.

There is an enormous amount of interest in the Old Testament around the way in which Israel related to the nations

At the same time, Israel was a nation among other nations in the broad sweep of Ancient Near Eastern macro-culture, and so there is considerable missiological interest in the variety of ways in which the faith of Israel related positively and negatively to the cultures of other nations over the centuries. For example, we could give much more missiological attention to the different responses of the patriarchal narratives to their surrounding culture; of the Deuteronomic materials to Canaanite culture; of the prophets to the relationship between Israel's experiment with royalty (king and temple) and Canaanite parallels; of the exilic and post-exilic communities to the world of Mesopotamian and Persian religion and culture; and these are just some of the possibilities.[7]

Later, covenantal obedience is not only based on Israel's historical redemption out of Egypt, but also linked to their identity and the major point of interest here is, in its shortest expression, the missiological dimension of Israel's holiness. Israel was called to be distinctive from the surrounding world in ways that were not merely religious but also ethical. This is expressed as the very purpose of their election in relation to God's promise to bless the nations in Genesis 18.19. In the context of, and in stark contrast to, the world of Sodom and Gomorrah, Yahweh says of Abraham, 'I have chosen him so that he will direct his children and his household after him to keep the way of the LORD by doing what is right and just, so that the LORD will bring about for Abraham what he has promised him.' This verse, in a remarkably tight syntax, binds together election, ethics and mission as three interlocking aspects of God's purpose. His choice of Abraham is for the sake of his promise (to bless the nations); but the accomplishment of that demands the ethical obedience of his community — the fulcrum in the middle of the verse.

Later, covenantal obedience is not only based on Israel's historical redemption out of Egypt, but also linked to their identity and role as a priestly and holy people in the midst of the nations in Exodus 19.4–6. As Yahweh's priesthood, Israel would be the means by which God would be known to the nations and the means of bringing them to God (performing a function analogous to the role of Israel's own priests between God and the rest of the people). As a holy people, they would be ethically (as well as ritually) distinctive from the practices of surrounding nations. The moral and practical dimensions of such holy distinctiveness are spelled out in Leviticus 18–19. Such visibility would be a matter of observation and comment among the nations, and that expectation in itself was a strong motivation for keeping the law (Deut 4.6–8). The question of Israel's ethical obedience or ethical failure was not merely a matter between themselves and Yahweh, but was of major significance in relation to Yahweh's agenda for the nations (see Jer 4.1–2).

This missiological perspective on Old Testament ethics seems to me a fruitful approach to the age-old hermeneutical debate over whether and how the moral teaching given to Israel in the Old Testament (especially the law), has any authority or relevance to Christians. If, as I believe, it was given in order to shape Israel to be what they were called to be — a light to the nations, a holy priesthood — then it has a paradigmatic relevance to those who, in Christ, have inherited the same role in relation to the nations. In the Old as well as the New Testament, the ethical demand on those who claim to be God's people is determined by the mission with which they have been entrusted.

The ethical demand on those who claim to be God's people is determined by the mission with which they have been entrusted

Eschatological Vision—The Ingathering of Nations

Israel saw the nations (including themselves) as being subject to the sovereign rule of God in history—whether in judgment or in mercy. This is a dimension of the Old Testament faith that we need to get our minds around, since it does not sit very congenially with our tendency to a very individualistic and pietistic form of spirituality (compare Jer 18.1–10; Jonah). But Israel also thought of the nations as 'spectators' of all God's dealings with Israel—whether positively or negatively. That is, whether on the receiving end of God's deliverance or of the blows of his judgment, Israel lived on an open stage and the nations would draw their conclusions (Exodus 15.15; Deut 9.28; Ezekiel 36.16–23).

Eventually, however, and in a rather mysterious way, the nations could be portrayed as the beneficiaries of all that God had done in and for Israel, and even invited to rejoice, applaud and praise Yahweh the God of Israel (Psalm 47; 1 Kings 8.41–43; Psalm 67). And, most remarkable of all, Israel came to entertain the eschatological vision that there would be those of the nations who would not merely be joined to Israel, but would come to be identified as Israel, with the same names, privileges and responsibilities before God (Psalm 47.9; Isaiah 19.19–25; 56.2–8; 66.19–21; Zech 2.10–11; Amos 9.11–12).[8]

These texts are quite breathtaking in their universal scope. This is the dimension of Israel's prophetic heritage that most profoundly influenced the theological explanation and motivation of the gentile mission in the New Testament. It certainly underlies James' interpretation of the Christ-event and the success of the gentile mission in Acts 15 (quoting Amos 9.12). And it likewise inspired Paul's efforts as a practitioner and theologian of mission (for example Romans 15.7–16). And, as we saw earlier, it provided the theological shape for the gospels, all of which conclude with their various forms of the great commission—the sending of Jesus' disciples into the world of nations.

And finally, of course, we cannot omit the even wider vision that not only the nations, but also the whole creation will be included in God's purposes of redemption. For this God of Israel, of the nations, and of the world, declares himself to be creating a new heavens and a new earth, with a picture of a redeemed humanity living in safety, harmony and environmental peace within a renewed creation. Again, this is a portrait enthusiastically endorsed in the New Testament and sustains our hope today (Psalm 96.11–13; Isaiah 65.17–25; Romans 8.18–21; 2 Peter 3.13; Rev 21.1–5).

This God of Israel, of the nations, and of the world, declares himself to be creating a new heavens and a new earth

Questions for Reflection

What are the forces that challenge either the uniqueness or the universality of God in your society or context?

Does the community in which you are located experience the mission of the church as a blessing? In what ways?

How might we become more effective in being a blessing to those around us (individually and corporately)?

In what ways might our approach to ethics hinder our mission? How might we engage with ethical issues in such a way as to enable mission?

What might it mean, for individual Christians and churches, to be 'ethically visible'?

How does having an eschatological perspective affect the way we view mission?

Conclusion   6

Much more could be said, taking up other major themes of the Old Testament and reading them from the perspective of the missional purpose of God for his people and his world.

From this angle also individual stories, event, persons, institutions come to have an added significance. At least I trust this sketch may have touched on some of what Jesus had in mind when he asserted that the mission of bringing the good news of repentance and forgiveness in his name to the nations is nothing less than what is written in the Scriptures that pointed to himself.

Questions for Reflection

Where are these different aspects of mission—the uniqueness of God, the universality of God, blessing the nations, ethical visibility, eschatology—find expression in the ministry of Jesus as recorded in the gospels?

Where do they find expression in the life of the early church in Acts and the letters?

Which of these dimensions of mission find expression in your own commitment to mission, either for yourself or in your local church?

How has what you have read in this booklet challenged your own understanding of mission?

What would you like to change as a result in

    a. your church's expression of its commitment mission?

    b. yours and your church's practice of mission?

Bibliography

For Further Reading on the Bible and Mission

Ådna, J and Kvalbein, H (eds), *The Mission of the Early Church to Jews and Gentiles* (Tübingen: Mohr Siebeck, 2000)

Bauckham, R, *Bible and Mission: Christian Witness in a Postmodern World* (Carlisle: Paternoster/Grand Rapids: Baker, 2003)

— *God Crucified* (Carlisle: Paternoster/Grand Rapids: Eerdmans, 1999)

Beeby, H D, 'A Missional Approach to Renewed Interpretation' in C Bartholomew, C Greene and K Moeller (eds), *Renewing Biblical Interpretation* (Carlisle: Paternoster/Grand Rapids: Zondervan, 2000) pp 268–283

— *Canon and Mission* (Harrisburg, Pennsylvania: Trinity Press, 1999)

Billington, A, A N S Lane, and M Turner (eds), *Mission and Meaning: Essays Presented to Peter Cotterell* (Carlisle: Paternoster, 1995)

Blauw, J, *The Missionary Nature of the Church* (New York: McGraw Hill, 1962)

Bosch, D J, 'Hermeneutical Principles in the Biblical Foundation for Mission,' *Evangelical Review of Theology* 17 (1993) pp 437–451

Briggs, R S, 'The Uses of Speech-Act Theory in Biblical Interpretation,' *Currents in Theology and Mission* 9 (2001), 229–276

Brownson, J V, 'Speaking the Truth in Love: Elements of a Missional Hermeneutic' in G R Hunsberger and C Van Gelder (eds), *The Church between Gospel and Culture* (Grand Rapids: Eerdmans, 1996) pp 228–259

— *Speaking the Truth in Love: New Testament Resources for a Missional Hermeneutic* (Harrisburg, Pennsylvania: Trinity Press, 1998)

Brueggemann, W, *Theology of the Old Testament: Testimony, Dispute, Advocacy* (Minneapolis: Fortress, 1997)

Burnett, D, *God's Mission, Healing the Nations* (Carlisle: Paternoster, 1996).

Filbeck, D, *Yes, God of the Gentiles Too: The Missionary Message of the Old Testament* (Wheaton: Billy Graham Centre, Wheaton College, 1994)

Franks, M, 'Election, Pluralism, and the Missiology of Scripture in a Postmodern Age,' *Missiology* 26 (1998) pp 329–343

Goerner, H C, *Thus It Is Written* (Nashville: Broadman Press, 1971)

Groot, A de, 'One Bible and Many Interpretive Contexts: Hermeneutics in Missiology' in A Camps, L A Hoedemaker, and M R Spindler (eds), *Missiology: An Ecumenical Introduction* (Grand Rapids: Eerdmans, 1995)

Hedlund, R, *The Mission of the Church in the World* (Grand Rapids: Baker, 1991)

Hesselgrave, D J, 'A Missionary Hermeneutic: Understanding Scripture in the Light of World Mission,' *International Journal of Frontier Missions* 10 (1993) pp 17–20

Hoedemaker, L A, 'The People of God and the Ends of the Earth' in A Camps, L A Hoedemaker, and M R Spindler (eds), *Missiology: An Ecumenical Introduction* (Grand Rapids: Eerdmans, 1995)

Jenkins, P, *The Next Christendom: The Coming of Global Christianity* (Oxford: Oxford University Press, 2002)

Kaiser Jr, W C, *Mission in the Old Testament: Israel as a Light to the Nations* (Grand Rapids: Baker, 2000)

Kirk, J A, *What Is Mission? Theological Explorations* (London: Darton, Longman and Todd/Minneapolis: Fortress Press, 1999)

Koestenberger, A J , 'The Place of Mission in New Testament Theology: An Attempt to Determine the Significance of Mission within the Scope of the New Testament's Message as a Whole,' *Missiology* 27 (1999) pp 347–362

— and P T O'Brien, *Salvation to the Ends of the Earth: A Biblical Theology of Mission* (Leicester: Apollos, 2001)

LaGrand, J, *The Earliest Christian Mission to 'All Nations' in the Light of Matthew's Gospel* (Grand Rapids: Eerdmans, 1995)

Le Grys, A, *Origins of the Mission of the Early Church* (London: SPCK, 1999).

Martin-Achard, R, *A Light to the Nations: A Study of the Old Testament Conception of Israel's Mission to the World* (J P Smith (tr), Edinburgh and London: Oliver & Boyd, 1962)

Middleton, J R and B J Walsh, *Truth Is Stranger Than It Used to Be: Biblical Faith in a Postmodern Age* (London: SPCK/Downers Grove: Inter-Varsity Press, 1995)

Patrick, D, *The Rendering of God in the Old Testament* (Philadelphia: Fortress, 1981)

Ridder, R R de, *Discipling the Nations* (Grand Rapids: Baker, 1975)

Rowley, H H, *The Missionary Message of the Old Testament* (London: Carey Press, 1944)

Scobie, C H H, 'Israel and the Nations: An Essay in Biblical Theology,' *Tyndale Bulletin* 43 (1992) pp 283–305

Senior, D and C Stuhlmueller, *The Biblical Foundations for Mission* (London: SCM, 1983)

Soards, M L, 'Key Issues in Biblical Studies and Their Bearing on Mission Studies,' *Missiology* 24 (1996) pp 93–109

Spindler, M R, 'The Biblical Grounding and Orientation of Mission' in A Camps, L A Hoedemaker, and M R Spindler, *Missiology: An Ecumenical Introduction* (Grand Rapids: Eerdmans, 1995) pp 123–143

Stott, J, *The Contemporary Christian: An Urgent Plea for Double Listening* (Leicester: Inter-Varsity Press, 1992)

Taber, C R, 'Missiology and the Bible,' *Missiology* 11 (1983) pp 229–245

Van Engen, C, 'The Relation of Bible and Mission in Mission Theology' in C Van Engen, D S Gilliland, and P Piersonn (eds), *The Good News of the Kingdom* (Maryknoll: Orbis, 1993) pp 27–36

Walls, A F, *The Missionary Movement in Christian History: Studies in the Transmission of Faith* (Maryknoll: Orbis/Edinburgh: T & T Clark, 1996)

Wright, C J H, 'Christ and the Mosaic of Pluralisms: Challenges to Evangelical Missiology in the 21st Century' in Taylor (ed), *Global Missiology for the 21st Century: The Iguassu Dialogue* (Grand Rapids: Baker, 2000) pp 71–99

— 'Covenant: God's Mission through God's People' in J A Grant and

A I Wilson (eds), *The God of Covenant* (Leicester: Inter-Varsity Press, 2005) pp 54–78

— 'Future Trends in Mission' in C Bartholomew, R Parry, and A West (eds), *The Futures of Evangelicalism: Issues and Prospects* (Leicester: Inter-Varsity Press, 2003) pp 149–163

— 'Mission as a Matrix for Hermeneutics and Biblical Theology' in C Bartholomew, *et al* (eds), *Out of Egypt: Biblical Theology and Biblical Interpretation* (Carlisle: Paternoster/Grand Rapids: Zondervan, 2004) pp 102–143

— *Old Testament Ethics for the People of God* (Leicester: Inter-Varsity Press, 2004)

— *Walking in the Ways of the Lord: The Ethical Authority of the Old Testament* (Leicester: Inter-Varsity Press, 1995)

Wright, N T, *Jesus and the Victory of God* (London: SPCK, 1996)

— *The New Testament and the People of God* (London: SPCK, 1992)

Notes

1   Another curious thought: I could have done precisely the same job in a college in England, but that would not have been considered 'mission.'

2   C R Taber, 'Missiology and the Bible,' *Missiology* 11 (1983) p 232.

3   Marion Soards surveys four current issues in New Testament studies (first-century Judaism, the life of Jesus, Pauline theology, and the character of the early church), and shows how they are relevant to mission studies also. But he concludes with a converse comment in line with the point being made here, 'Mission studies should remind biblical scholars that many of the writings that we study (often in painstaking and even painful detail) came to be because of the reality of mission. An awareness of, and a concern with, the key issues of mission studies may well help biblical studies find foci that will bring deeper appreciation of the meaning of the Bible' — M L Soards, 'Key Issues in Biblical Studies and Their Bearing on Mission Studies,' *Missiology* 24 (1996) p 107. With this I fully agree. See also A J Koestenberger, 'The Place of Mission in New Testament Theology. An Attempt to Determine the Significance of Mission within the Scope of the New Testament's Message as a Whole,' *Missiology* 27 (1999) and the works referred to there.

4   A missiological hermeneutic of the Old Testament if ever there was one! As the NIV footnote shows, Paul has no problem applying the singular 'you' — which was spoken to the Servant — to the plural 'us.'

5   David Bosch, *Transforming Mission* (Maryknoll, 1991). The relevant words are, 'There is, in the Old Testament, no indication of the believers of the old covenant being sent by God to cross geographical, religious, and social frontiers in order to win others to faith in Yahweh...Even so, the Old Testament is fundamental to the understanding of mission in the New' (p 17).

6   This has been shown very clearly, and in a way which underlines its importance for the whole mission of the biblical God through the people of God for the world, in the works of N T Wright, especially his *The New Testament and the People of God* (London, 1992) pp 244–79, and *Jesus and the Victory of God* (London, 1996).

7   Walter Brueggemann is one of very few Old Testament scholars who have given serious and detailed attention to the nations as a theological reality in the Old Testament. See *Theology of the Old Testament: Testimony, Dispute, Advocacy* (Minneapolis, 1997) pp 492–527.

8   See Acts 15.16–18; Eph 2.11–3.6.